CW00819939

The Beauty of
ADDIS ABABA

Graham Hancock

Photographs by
Mohamed Amin and Duncan Willetts

Camerapix Publishers International

First published 1995 by
Camerapix Publishers International,
P. O. Box 45048,
Nairobi,
Kenya

© Camerapix 1995

Second impression 1997

This book was designed and produced by
Camerapix Publishers International,
P.O. Box 45048,
Nairobi,
Kenya

ISBN 1 87404113 X

Edited by Brian Tetley

*Half-title: Church of Archangel Raguel in Addis Ababa, built in 1995 on the site of
the house of Hapte Georgis, war minister to Menelik II. Title page: View of the city
of Addis Ababa from the Entoto foothills. Contents page: Evening sunlight dusts
the buildings of Addis with pure gold. Pages 6-7: Statue of Menelik II, the city's
founder, in the centre of Menelik II Square, Addis Ababa.*

Printed and bound in Singapore by Tien Wah Press Pte Ltd

Contents

Introduction

Wide tree-lined streets, fine architecture, glorious weather and well-mannered drivers make Addis Ababa, the capital of Ethiopia, a delightful place to explore — a city of surprises characterised by remarkable diversity and contrasts.

Abundant eucalyptus trees and crisp, clear mountain air endow this African capital with the bracing, pine-scented atmosphere of a highland summer resort. Its cosy espresso bars and patisseries are reminiscent of Rome and the Mediterranean and its bustling outdoor markets are colourful reminders of more traditional ways of life. The people, the bursts of music from cafes or shops, the pungent aromas of spicy cooking, of coffee and frankincense, form a unique Ethiopian pastiche and the architecture is as varied as the city itself. Tall skyscrapers, elegant villas, functional bungalows, flats and condominiums gleaming in their marble and anodised aluminium vie for attention alongside traditional homes of wattle and daub, surrounded by cattle, sheep, goats, chickens, conference halls, and theatres.

Vibrant Addis Ababa is as cosmopolitan as any of the world's great metropolises. There is no designated city-centre because, until very recently, there was no urban planning. Addis Ababa simply grew in a natural, organic way — and its present appearance reflects this unforced and unstructured evolution.

Set in rising countryside between 2,200 and 2,500 metres above sea level and dominated by the 3,000-metres-high Entoto mountains immediately to the north, Ethiopia's largest city has grown at astonishing speed since it was founded just over a century ago. Covering 250 square kilometres, it rambles pleasantly across many wooded hillsides and gullies cut through with fast-flowing streams. Despite its proximity to the

Equator its lofty altitude — it is the third-highest capital in the world — means that it enjoys a mild, Afro-Alpine climate with an average temperature of 16°C. The hottest, driest months are April and May. The rainy season, which tourists are well advised to avoid, is from July to September.

In the dry season the days are pleasantly warm and the nights cool. During the rainy season days and nights are cool, by local standards. Visitors coming from the cold European winter, however, will probably find Addis Ababa's climate ideal and light clothing for daytime wear, with a jersey and jacket available for evenings, should suffice.

Although Addis Ababa has only recently entered its second century, in a sense it can legitimately claim a distinguished and ancient pedigree that stretches back more than 2,000 years. The latest in a long line of capital cities, its brash newness is tempered by the inheritance of wisdom, sophistication and experience handed down to it by its predecessors.

The earliest capital that Ethiopia has known during its long and turbulent history, founded at least 2,500 years ago, was located in the far north of the country — at Yeha, in Tigray, where a great stone temple of pre-Christian times can still be seen.

The next capital to emerge was the important political, commercial and religious city of Axum, south-west of Yeha. Axum was the capital of Ethiopia throughout much of the first millennium of the Christian era. The city is the site of many fine stone stelae. One of these monolithic towers, which still stands, rises to a height of more than twenty-one metres and is carved to represent a building of nine storeys. It tapers slightly towards the summit and is crowned by a graceful headpiece

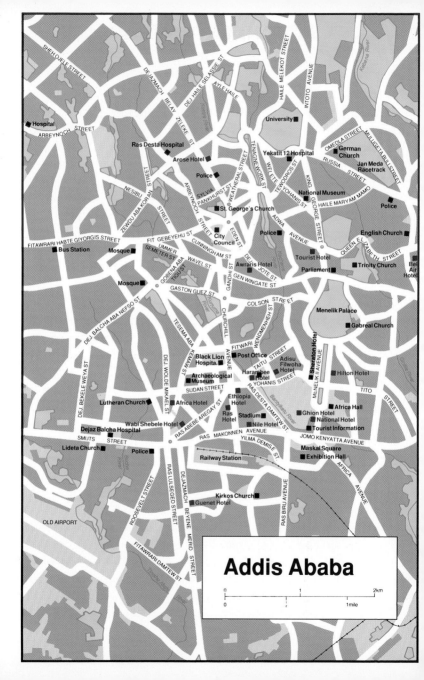

Addis Ababa

0	1	2km
0	1mile	

thought by some to represent the sun. Henry Salt, a British traveller first saw it in 1805. "My attention was for a long time riveted on this beautiful and extraordinary monument." Five years later he declared: "It made nearly as forcible an impression upon my mind as at the first moment I beheld it." Other antiquities in the city include the remains of several ancient palaces as well as subterranean tombs built, like almost everything in Axum, of hard granite. Another remarkable building is the great church of St Mary of Zion, a seventeenth-century structure erected on the site of a much older edifice believed to have been founded not long after Axum's adoption of Christianity as the state religion in the fourth century AD. Axum, in fact, is an archaeological paradise, and each year after the rains the local farmers and their sharp-eyed children find dozens of gold, silver and bronze coins in the fields in and around the city.

Lalibela, in the mountains of Lasta, is believed to have come into existence after the decline of Axum in the tenth century. Originally called Roha, and the capital of a local dynasty known as the Zagwe, the settlement was renamed Lalibela after its most important ruler who lived in the late twelfth and early thirteenth centuries. The town is renowned for its eleven remarkable rock-hewn churches which are thought to have been built during Lalibela's rule and which have been ranked among the wonders of the world. The Portuguese traveller Francisco Alvarez, who visited there in 1520, described them as edifices, the like of which — and so many — cannot be found anywhere else in the world. Explaining that they were entirely excavated in the rock, and were very well hewn he added: "It wearies me to write more of these works, because it seems to me that they will not believe me, if I write more."

Despite the existence of these, and other cities, urbanisation in the middle ages was hampered by the absence of a fixed capital. The rulers of that period travelled with their courts and armies from one military camp to another, and did so, as the chronicle of the sixteenth century Emperor Galawdewos observed, "until their last resting place."

The middle ages nonetheless witnessed the founding in the sixteenth century of the notable city of Harar in the east of the country. This settlement, which was inhabited solely by Muslims, was unique in that its population spoke a language, Adare, not known anywhere else. The city, like Axum so many centuries earlier, issued its own currency. A notable event in the history of Harar was the building by Emir Nur, a mid-sixteenth-century ruler, of the sturdy surrounding walls which still stand. They were pierced, as the eminent British orientalist Richard Burton who visited the city in the mid-nineteenth century noted, by five large gates . . . supported by oval towers. Harar, the principal commercial emporium on the Horn of Africa, boasted many mosques and Muslim shrines, and was noted for its handicrafts. According to Burton these included celebrated cloths, as well as finely bound manuscripts which "no Eastern country save Persia surpasses in strength and appearance."

The shift of political power to the north-west of Ethiopia in the late sixteenth century led to the emergence of a succession of capitals in that part of the country. The first was at Emfraz, also known as Guzara, where Emperor Sartsa Dengel built a strong fortress which still stands. Castle-based towns were later also established at Gorgora on the northern shore of Lake Tana, and at Danqaz a little further to the north.

The most important capital of this period, however, was

Above: Ceremonial bathing place of Emperor Fasilidas - used for baptisms during Timkat.

Right: Mosque in Harar.

Left: Axum stelae dating back to the 1st or 2nd centuries AD. *The tallest still standing is nine storeys and 23 metres high.*

Gondar, established by Emperor Fasilidas in 1636. It remained the capital of Ethiopia for more than two centuries and was, in its day, a major emporium as well as a religious centre with over forty churches. The city today is best known for its famous crenellated castles which were first described by the eighteenth-century Scottish explorer James Bruce. He wrote of the principal building, erected by Fasilidas, as a structure of considerable consequence with a magnificent view of all the country southwards as far as Lake Tana.

In the centuries which followed, numerous other cities emerged in various parts of the country. Among the earliest of these settlements was Adwa in Tigray, which was the principal commercial centre between Gondar and the Red Sea port of Massawa; Sekota, the capital of the district of Wag; Bonga, a sometime capital of Kaffa in the south-west of the country; and Ankober in Shoa.

Many other provincial capitals likewise came into existence in the early nineteenth century, among them Debre Tabor in Begemder, Antalo and Adigrat in Tigray, Bichena and Dima in Gojjam, and Angolala and Debra Berhan in Shoa.

The last half of the nineteenth century and the first decades of the twentieth, which were notable for the foundation and growth of Addis Ababa, were also marked by the founding of scores of other towns, the most important of which are today modern cities. Among all, however, only Addis Ababa attained the stature of a true capital.

1. Ethiopia's New Flower

Addis Ababa, today one of Africa's largest cities with a population of around three million, and the continent's premier diplomatic centre as the headquarters of the Organization of African Unity, is extremely young in fact by Ethiopian standards. In this land, where history seems to stretch back almost without limit into the remote and legendary past, it seems a brash newcomer. Located in a happy valley surrounded by lofty mountains, it was founded not much more than a century ago by Emperor Menelik II, the great moderniser of Ethiopia. Though it is hard to believe when confronted by the concrete reality of this burgeoning metropolis, where skyscrapers now rise and traffic moves ceaselessly along wide, tree-lined avenues, pleasant meadows once stretched and hot springs burbled.

It was in the late 1870s when Menelik began to show an interest in the region where Addis Ababa is situated, headquartering the royal camp at several sites in the area. His first major settlement was established on the slopes of Mount Wuchacha, west of the present capital, but he soon moved northwards to set up his camp near the summit of Entoto — the mountain which overlooks modern Addis Ababa from the north.

The event that precipitated this move came in 1881 when the ruins of an old town — believed to have been the capital of the revered sixteenth-century monarch Lebna Dengel — were discovered at Entoto. Menelik at once visited the site, and exclaimed: "God has caused us to find the remains of the city of Entoto. Since this discovery has been made in our time it is incumbent on us to resurrect the city." He transferred his camp to the old site, and gave instructions that a new city should be built there.

Above: A scene almost typical of the brush of the artist van Gogh, Entoto as seen from the far side of Addis.

Opposite top: At Entoto, the octagonal Church of the Archangel Raguel.

Opposite: Church of Maryam, Entoto.

19

Entoto's initial character was mainly that of a large military camp — with a population of not less than 50,000 from the outset. Like most Ethiopian capitals of the past it was strategically well situated, for it stood on an easily defensible mountain, and was surrounded by a deep trench, part of which is still visible. Moreover, the Entoto range was located at the watershed between the Blue Nile basin to the north and that of the Awash river to the south, and thus provided easy access to most of central Ethiopia.

Initially the settlement consisted principally of tents, but before long many buildings had been constructed. The first was a timber palace for Menelik built by a master carpenter and nine assistants from Gondar. Menelik's Swiss adviser and craftsman, Alfred Ilg, and two other Swiss workmen, were also employed on the building.

The next important building at Entoto was the church of Maryam, a circular structure, the foundations of which were laid in 1885. Menelik is said to have taken part in the building work — on occasion travelling with his consort Queen Taytu to Mount Managesha, in the west, where he helped to prepare the church's massive squared roof beams which were carried dozens of kilometres by groups of four or five soldiers. It was in this church of Maryam that Menelik was crowned Emperor of Ethiopia in November 1889, and an effigy of the old monarch hangs on its walls.

While the church was being built, the foundations were being dug for another place of worship dedicated to the archangel Raguel. This stone church, which lay within the palace compound, was designed by an Indian craftsman, Haji Khawas of Peshawar, and it was unusual in being octagonal, not round as was then customary. It had a first-floor balustrade which Menelik often walked around on ceremonial occasions.

Entoto expanded rapidly for several years. The site which had initially been selected as a fortress, however, was unsuitable as a capital for more peaceful times. Standing on a rugged mountain it was poorly supplied. Provisions were brought up by way of an exhausting walk and food and water was often scarce. Wood was also difficult to obtain. Moreover, Entoto's climate during the rainy season was far from pleasant, for it suffered from many storms. A French traveller, Jules Borelli, states that it was a place of much lightning, thunder and fog, while his compatriot, Charles Michel, complained that the town was an impossible capital, exposed to the wind, difficult of access and without drinking water.

Because of the inclement weather on Entoto, Menelik and Queen Taytu rode down a number of times to sojourn on the nearby plain of Finefine, which lay to the south. It was also known as *Filwoha* — Amharic for hot spring — on account of the thermal springs which bubbled out of the ground there. Menelik's court paid its first visit to the spot in 1885. In the following year Queen Taytu, admiring the beauty of the scenery of *Filwoha* from the door of her tent, and pleased with the mildness of the climate, is said to have asked her husband for land on which to build a proper house. He allocated an area above the hot springs and building is reported to have begun within a week. One year later, during the rains of 1887, she installed herself there and allotted land around the royal camp to all the chiefs in accordance with traditional practice, and they began to build their own houses. Taytu named the new settlement *Addis Ababa*, literally New Flower, perhaps on account of the flowering mimosa trees then prevalent in the

area. Work on a palace for Menelik began early in 1889, some months before his coronation as Emperor, and the first stone buildings were erected in 1891.

Menelik's original palace at Addis Ababa was accidentally destroyed by fire in 1892 but soon rebuilt. No fewer than fifty structures in the palace compound were erected within three months and, by 1894, the entire palace compound was virtually restored.

One innovation was the installation of piped water to the palace, a scheme conceived and executed by Menelik's Swiss aide, Alfred Ilg. It created considerable excitement. The palace, as the craftsman's biographer Conrad Keller explains, had no water supply and, when the Swiss proposed to tap a spring on a neighbouring hill by a system of pipes, many courtiers declared the idea impossible. They argued that although water could be conveyed to the bottom of a hill, it could never run up it.

But Menelik, always interested in technological innovations, was convinced, and the pipes were laid according to Ilg's plan. When the water was first turned on it failed to flow. Ilg ran all along the pipe, tapping each section until he traced the fault. One section had been stuffed with cotton seed — apparently an act of sabotage by an Ethiopian friend who often visited his house. When the blockage was removed the water gushed out and the scheme was acclaimed a marvel. A contemporary poem declared:

We have seen wonders in Addis Ababa
Water worships Emperor Menelik
O Menelik, what more wisdom will you bring?
You already make water soar into the air!

Several more buildings were later erected in the palace

compound, among them the Church of Gabriel built by a group of Indian masons and finely painted by Ethiopian artists.

The most impressive structure, however, was the large *adarash*, or reception hall, completed in 1897. Menelik's chronicler, Gabre Selassie, who describes the building as altogether extraordinary, states that it measured 120 cubits long by sixty wide and had a three-gabled roof covering a single hall. Inside this room sixteen clusters of electric lights — themselves a notable innovation in Ethiopia — were suspended from the ceiling. They illuminated the halls so brightly, it is claimed, that people were dazzled as by the rays of the sun. Further light entered on the east side through three stained-glass windows with red, green, yellow and blue panes, as well as through two windows above the doors, and another two on the west wall. There were other multi-coloured windows on the north and south walls, all, it is said, very beautiful. The roof was supported by no less than thirty-four pillars painted in various colours — so many uprights being required, Gabre Selassie claims, to support so large a structure. The gables were fitted with gutters, yet another innovation. When it rained water poured off them in a great, noisy torrent.

The size of the *adarash* was a source of immense pride. The hall could hold 6,987 persons — not counting the chiefs to the right and left of the monarch, his favourites, who stood at the corners of the throne according to their rank, and the 300 or so officials who distributed meat, bread and mead at court banquets.

In those years, and indeed later, the palace was the setting for huge state banquets. Amazed foreign travellers told of meals attended in several sessions by up to 5,000 guests at a

Above: Menelik Monument at Menelik Hospital, Addis Ababa.

Opposite top: Lion of Judah Monument, Addis Ababa, near the railway station.
Opposite left: Face in relief of Menelik II on one of the four sides of the Lion Monument.
Opposite right: Face in relief of Ras Tafari Makonnen, subsequently Emperor Haile Selassie.

time. No invitation cards were issued, nor was there any question of payment: anyone came who wished, whatever his status, ethnic origin or religion, be he freeman or slave, Christian or Jew, Muslim or pagan.

The palace compound, as the governmental and military headquarters of a country just beginning to embark on technical progress, struck outsiders in Menelik's day as a remarkably complex and multi-faceted establishment. The nerve centre of a vast empire, it was frequented by all men of state and was the site of much political, ceremonial and diplomatic activity. Because of the scarcity of modern skills in Ethiopia, it was also the location of workshops of all kinds. It was thus — as Dr George Merab — a Georgian resident of the time asserts, a microcosm of the kingdom, an almost self-sufficient realm with its own agricultural and industrial resources — a state, a farm and a series of factories and workshops all rolled into one.

Within the palace compound, which measured two kilometres long by one-and-a-half kilometres wide, were structures of every possible shape and size: the *adarash*, where the banquets were held; the private and secluded apartments of Menelik and Taytu; the *shakla bet*, the first building in the city ever constructed of brick; dwellings of most unusual oriental design (some with zinc roofs) side by side with traditional, circular thatched mud huts; the Ministry or Council Chamber; the treasury; a court of law; several churches; post and telegraph offices; jewellers and embroiderers' booths and weavers' workshops; a saddlery; a smithy; a joinery; an arms, gunpowder and cartridge store — the beginnings of an arsenal; the mint to hold the new currency that Menelik had just introduced; a pharmacy and adjacent dispensary; stables; vegetable gardens; a small forest; flower beds and haystacks; meadows and ploughed lands planted with hops, vines, cabbages and celery; a meeting place for lost mules and runaway slaves; fresh springs for water and murmuring streams; cellars for mead and beer; thick-walled store rooms for silver dollars; latrines for the numerous personnel; herds of cattle and sheep fattening up for forthcoming banquets; many guards; groups of beggars; a lion-house and menagerie complete with a couple of lions, two or three ostriches and a dozen or so hornbills. The whole establishment employed about 8,000 people, some 2,000 of whom were in the personal service of the Emperor and his consort.

Menelik's victory over an invading Italian army at Adwa in northern Ethiopia on 1 March 1896, a decade after the founding of Addis Ababa, was followed by renewed growth of the capital and Italian prisoners of war were put to work in and around the city — especially in road building. During this period Saint George's church, the capital's second place of worship, was built. It was a round building in traditional style with a thatched roof, not to be confused with the octagonal structure which later took its place.

To the south of Saint George's, on slightly lower ground, lay the original Addis Ababa market, since relocated at a more westerly site. At the turn of the century, it occupied a stretch of land 1,000 metres long by 200 to 300 metres wide, and was attended each day by thousands of people. On Saturdays close to 50,000 shoppers and vendors flocked there. The British big-game hunter and ethnographer, P.H.G. Powell-Cotton, who visited the market a century ago, noted that to it came grains and spices, peppers and condiments, from every corner of the

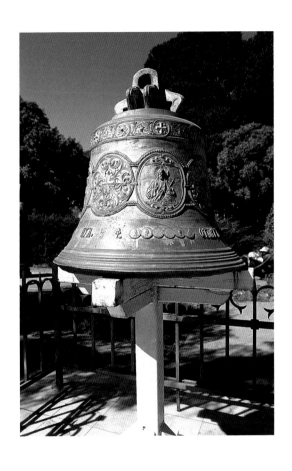

Above: Made by the Russians prior to the Bolshevic Revolution, St George's Cathedral bell.

Opposite: St George's Cathedral where Haile Selassie was crowned.

kingdom, coffee from Harar and Lake Tana, cotton from the banks of the Blue Nile, gold from Beni Shangul, and civet from Galla country, while salt from the far north of Tigray was the current change for the dollar. Fine cotton *shammas* (or togas), heavy burnouses of black, blanket-like cloth, jewellery and arms, saddlery and ploughs, were all there. In fact there you could feel the commercial pulse of Abyssinia, gain some insight into the present state of her civilisation, and gather what she had to offer in exchange.

Despite the presence of the palace, the churches and the market, Addis Ababa in Menelik's day was essentially a rural settlement, a character which — even with its modern expansion — it still retains to some extent in the 1990s, rambling over a vast area, with meadows and grazing grounds interspersed between high-rise and government buildings. "What struck me most," wrote the English traveller and author Sir Alfred Pease in 1899, "was the absence of anything in the nature of a town as we understand it, and the extraordinary way in which the population is scattered over the valley; single huts here, bunches of huts there, white tents pitched in groups."

The picture was confirmed by Powell-Cotton who remarked that dotted about the plain were clusters of huts, many stockaded enclosures — large and small — and several camps, but all very much scattered and more resembling a collection of villages and farmsteads than the capital of a great empire.

Movement within the settlement was far from easy — particularly during the rainy season. "In the summer rains," observed Pease, "people are entirely cut off from one another, and at all times of the year communication is difficult, partly because the distances are long, and partly because the track winds up and down the water courses, so it takes a long time to move from place to place." Another Englishman, Herbert Vivian, no less graphically declared: "Streets there are none, and to go from one part of town to the other you must simply bestride your mule and prepare to ride across country. Three quarters of an hour at least are necessary for a pilgrimage from the British Agency to the Palace, and as much again to the market. On either of these journeys you must cross three or four deep ravines with stony, precipitous banks and a torrent-bed full of slippery boulders."

The extensive use of timber for buildings and palisades, as well as the immense consumption of firewood for heating and cooking, and the absence of afforestation, soon led to an acute shortage of wood in Addis Ababa. "For two or three days before reaching the capital," wrote Vivian, "we had to do without wood in camp, for there was scarcely a tree to be seen." Every shrub that could possibly be used for firing had been cleared.

This dearth of wood was so great that late nineteenth-century foreign observers were convinced that Menelik would be obliged to abandon Addis Ababa, and leave it to fade into insignificance like Entoto before it. A.B. Wylde, a not unsympathetic British traveller who visited the capital in 1897, observed that the immmense, straggling settlement had seen its best days and that some new place would have to be chosen as the Emperor's headquarters, for it was by then impossible to procure firewood for the wants of the inhabitants. In fact, Addis Ababa, he was convinced, was doomed. Count Gleichen, a British envoy, agreed, declaring: "Sooner or later a new spot must be chosen, for gradually all the wood is being cut down and consumed, and when the

Above: Haile Selassie's Jubilee Palace, Addis Ababa.
Left: Haile Selassie's office in the Jubilee Palace.

Opposite: Impressive Main State Room on the ground floor of Haile Selassie's Palace — his throne can be seen in the background.

distance from the forest becomes inconveniently great, the capital must be removed elsewhere."

Indeed, Menelik was so concerned by the shortage of wood that he contemplated moving the capital from Addis Ababa. In the autumn of 1900 he made his way forty kilometres to the west where he started work on a new settlement which was later called *Addis Alem*, literally New World.

The building of Addis Alem was carried out with remarkable speed. There are accounts of as many as 20,000 local peasants being used as labourers. Pavilions, houses and an *adarash* were put up, according to Lincoln de Castro, a doctor at the Italian legation, in the briefest time, and work was soon in progress on a large rectangular palace building.

The Viscount Bourg du Bozas' mission commented early in 1902 that Addis Alem was the town of the future, as Addis Ababa was that of the present, and Entoto that of the past. The Italians were so impressed with this idea that, anxious to win Menelik's favour, and to regain prestige lost at the Battle of Adwa less than half a decade earlier, they decided to move to the new town. They therefore began work there on a legation building which a visiting French mission, led by Jean Duchesne-Fournet, described as one of the finest, if not actually the finest, in the country.

The proposed move to Addis Alem, however, encountered strong opposition — notably from persons who had already invested in costly structures in Addis Ababa, including not only the Ethiopian nobility but also foreign legations. For example, the British envoy, John Harrington, testily complained to the Foreign Office in 1902 that, if the capital were transferred to the new settlement, one would have to build another Agency there, with the possible result that as soon as the representatives had their residences there the King would think the time had come for building another Addis something. The prospect of having to keep up two separate and distinct establishments, and of flitting to and fro between them, was not attractive.

Opposition also came from Empress Taytu, who is said by de Castro to have declared that the palace at Addis Ababa was the best in the country and that there was therefore no need of any other.

Though Ethiopia had a long tradition of moving capitals there were strong reasons for remaining in Addis Ababa. Vast resources had been ploughed into the development of the existing capital. Moreover, work was in progress on a railway link to the port of Djibouti to the east, and any deviation of the line would be fraught with difficulties. Another factor of great importance was the advent of the quick-growing eucalyptus tree known in Amharic as *bahr-zaf*, or overseas tree, which was introduced from Australia. The first of these were probably planted by a Frenchman, Casimir Mondon-Vidailhet, who was followed by the Swiss craftsman Ilg and a French trader, Leon Chefneux. The tree was an immediate success: after five years it reached a height of more than twelve metres, and by the time it was twelve years old it was fifteen or twenty metres tall. Eucalyptus trees were soon being planted by the hectare, with the result that the capital, which Wylde had described as nearly treeless, was within a decade or two referred to by Merab as a Eucalyptopolis, or town of eucalyptus trees. These trees still contribute greatly to the charm and fragrance of the Ethiopian capital.

It is no exaggeration to say that the introduction of the eucalyptus tree played a major role in the future of Ethiopia in

Above: St Mary's Church, also known as Debre Zion Church, at Addis Alem. At almost 100 years old, it is one of the oldest churches in the Addis Ababa area and was built by Indian craftsmen.

Opposite: Ornate door of the church of Debre Zion.

that it solved Addis Ababa's chronic shortage of wood, and thereby assured the permanency of the city. Inevitably, the plan to transfer the capital to Addis Alem was abandoned. Taytu, referring to the still uncompleted palace building there, is said to have observed to her husband: "It is better that this structure become a church in order that it may serve us as a guide to the Kingdom of Heaven." Acceding to her arguments Menelik rode in 1902 to the new settlement and, declaring that the Kingdom of Heaven was worth more than the Kingdom on earth, gave orders that the building should be converted into a place of worship. It was accordingly dedicated to Saint Mary. This building, originally conceived as a palace but now a church, stands only an hour's drive from Addis Ababa, and is connected to the capital by a road which Menelik built in 1902. This road was the first such highway in the whole country.

During Menelik's rule, Addis Ababa was the site of many innovations. Foreign travellers at the turn of the century were constantly commenting on signs of progress in the capital. Powell-Cotton, for example, describes the telegraph station as being built in the form of a large circular *tukul*, or hut, the roofs supported inside by a ring of posts, on which hung the rifles and shields of the guard. Though placed in this traditional setting, the office was well-equipped, for the visitor could find the latest inventions in telegraphic and telephonic apparatus lying on tables of rough packing-cases, side by side with a few *amole* (bars of slat) and piles of cartridge cases (both empty and full), which had been received in payment for the messages sent.

Other innovations in the first years of the twentieth century included a 2,400-metre racecourse, inaugurated in 1903; the first bank — the Bank of Abyssinia — founded in 1906; the first hotel, the Etege, in 1907; the first modern school, the Menelik School, in 1908; and the capital's first hospital, the Menelik Hospital, in 1910. A state printing press was established in 1911, and a hydroelectric installation came into operation on the nearby Akaki river some months later. Attempts were also made to set up a cinema. Initially, however, it met with much disfavour and was often spoken of as *Seytan-bet*, or House of Satan.

The last years of Menelik's reign also witnessed a considerable amount of building, both public and private. One of the finest structures from this period is the cathedral of Saint George, an octagonal building designed by a Greek architect, Orphanides, and built by an Italian engineer, Castagna.

Many private homes were also put up — 14,000 by 1912. The vast majority, however, were only mud huts, although about 200 were stone.

The capital's first brick factory was established in 1907, and four others — one owned by the Italian, Castagna, and three others by Greeks — came into production in the next few years. Meanwhile corrugated-iron roofing had begun to be imported soon after the Djibouti railway reached Dire Dawa in 1902 and by 1906 no fewer than 50,000 sheets were sold every year.

Several well-made roads were also in existence by 1903. The American envoy, Robert Skinner, saw an excellent macadamised track leading to the British legation and wrote with enthusiasm of the smooth and well-built roads along which Menelik was introducing modern civilisation. In the following year the first steamroller arrived, brought to

42

Above: Wood Palace built by Shiek Hojélé.

Opposite top: Addis Ababa Railway Station.
Opposite below: Addis Ababa Museum, former home of Ras Biru Wolde Gabriel.

Ethiopia by an Armenian, Sarkis Terzian. It was thereafter constantly at work.

Two wooden bridges were built by French carpenters at the end of the nineteenth century, and the first stone bridge — by Russian engineers — in 1902 after one of them drowned swimming across a swollen river.

The continued growth of the city, and the arrival of many foreigners brought significant change in eating and drinking habits. Several corn mills and bakeries were in operation early in the twentieth century. A decade or so later numerous butchers' shops sprang up — a notable innovation in that Ethiopians traditionally slaughtered their own livestock. By 1913 the capital could boast two or three restaurants and as many cafes, mainly Greek-owned, as well as two hotels and no fewer than 100 *tej* (mead) drinking houses — the number of which soon increased tenfold.

Significant changes in fashion followed the advent of the sewing machine after the American firm Singer opened a branch in Addis Ababa in 1909. Soon they were selling hundreds of machines for 150 Maria Theresa dollars each, payable over many months.

These, and similar developments in other fields, testified to the fact that Addis Ababa had become the capital of a country with modern aspirations. By the time that Menelik's rule ended in 1913 the city had a population of around 100,000, the largest market in the whole of Ethiopia, and fortifications which enclosed an area equal to Paris.

An important event in Addis Ababa's history was the 1917 completion of the railway line from Djibouti, greatly improving communications and trade with the outside world. The years which followed also witnessed a steady increase in the number of motor cars — the first of which had arrived in Menelik's day. By 1928 there were at least 500 vehicles in the capital and the first traffic police were appointed about this time. The first airport also dates from this period.

New modern buildings included several schools and hospitals and the 1929 railway station, as well as the late Emperor's palace — now Addis Ababa University — and the Institute of Ethiopian Studies' fine Ethnological Museum, now a notable tourist attraction.

A solid mausoleum for Menelik and Taytu was built within the palace compound in 1930, and the parliament building (now an important Government office) was completed in 1934. Two cinemas and a well-frequented nightclub also came into existence.

But the Italian invasion in 1935, and subsequent five-year occupation, brought great hardship to the citizens of Addis Ababa and Ethiopians in general. Faced with the imminent occupation of the capital, at the beginning of May 1936, a group of Ethiopian nationalists attempted to set fire to the city to prevent it from falling into the hands of the enemy — as the Russians a century earlier had destroyed Moscow to deny it to Napoleon's army. Much of the commercial centre was destroyed.

After seizing the city the Italians established a large occupation force. Initially, however, they were reluctant to build, for they wanted to transfer the capital to flatter, less-elevated land. Building was therefore limited to a number of prefabricated, portable buildings, mainly of wood. On the other hand, there was a considerable amount of road building, which was urgently needed whichever capital was chosen. Eventually it was decided to retain Addis Ababa and, indeed,

Above: Ethiopian Airlines Boeing 737 refuelling at Addis Ababa Airport.

Opposite: Statue in Addis Ababa of Abuna Petros, an Ethiopian bishop martyred by the Italian fascists in 1936.

to make it the centre of government of a vast Italian empire embracing the entire Horn of Africa.

The occupation was vigorously opposed by Ethiopian patriots, some of whom worked secretly within the capital while others operated freely in nearby mountains as well as throughout much of the rest of the country. Resistance forces launched two attacks on the city — both in the summer of 1936 — but were unable to recapture it. Their attacks led to many reprisals including the public execution of an Ethiopian bishop, Abuna Petros, a statue of whom was later to be raised on the site. In February 1937 an attempt on the life of the fascist viceroy, Graziani, by two Eritreans, Abraha Debotch and Mogos Asgedom, provoked the Italians to unleash a three-day reign of terror during which thousands of unarmed Ethiopian citizens were murdered in cold blood and many houses were burnt down. Undeterred by such massacre and many other acts of repression, the Ethiopian resistance refused to abandon the struggle, which continued throughout the entire period of fascist rule.

Having decided to retain Addis Ababa as the capital, the Italians began a grandiose building programme, conceived — as they proclaimed in fascist terms — with a view to creating a metropolis with an anticipated European population of 200,000. Italians were to settle to the east and south of the city while Ethiopians were to be relegated to the west, and two complete residential neighbourhoods were constructed for the exclusive use of Italians. One, for officials, was built by a parastatal organisation, the grandly named *Instituto Nazionale per le Case degli Impiegati dello Stato.* To this day the area is known as Casa INCIS. The other, for Italian workers, is spoken of as Casa Popolari. Ethiopians in the areas designated for Europeans were evicted and moved to the west of the city. The main market, which had been situated below Saint George's Cathedral since Menelik's day, was also shifted west to its present location — an area sometimes referred to as *Addis Ketema* (or New Town), but most frequently known simply as the Mercato. Indian merchants, who until then had been prominent in the city's trade, were victimised because of their British connections and for the most part expelled.

The occupation also witnessed a number of imposing concrete buildings, mainly for governmental or parastatal use, as well as the establishment of a temporary airport, with wooden structures, and the excavation of two water reservoirs outside the city — at Gafarsa to the west and Abba Samuel to the east. Much use was made of the prewar buildings, among them schools and hospitals, which were now put into service for the benefit of Italians rather than Ethiopians. Yet at the collapse of the fascist occupation in 1940 most Italian structures were no more than blueprints. Indeed the Governor's office was in the former Emperor's palace.

Mussolini's entry into the European war in June 1940 led Britain to destroy Italian power in East Africa. Fascist rule in Addis Ababa finally ended in April 1941, and the city's temporary Italian population was repatriated, the colour bar lifted, and the old Ethiopian Government restored. Subsequently, several streets were renamed in honour of Allied wartime leaders and commanders.

The years which followed witnessed the establishment, or re-establishment, in the city of various ministries and government institutions, as well as of a number of foreign companies and, later, offices of international organisations.

The capital's architecture began to change in the late 1950s

Above: The house of Shaka Belehu, a prominent courtier of former times.

Opposite: Menelik Mausoleum built in 1930.

and early 1960s, with the construction of much larger and more modern buildings. The first of these was the new Arts building of Addis Ababa University College, now part of Addis Ababa University's Faculty of Science, a five-storey building, with continuous bands of windows, designed by C.A. Fallek, a British architect. This fine structure, which created considerable excitement when it was first erected, was soon outclassed by many even larger buildings — among them Africa Hall, headquarters of the UN's Economic Commission for Africa, and the Addis Ababa City Hall in a particularly imposing location at the top of Churchill Road. Other buildings of interest from this period include the Jubilee Palace, now called the National Palace, and the nearby Hilton Hotel which boasts a large cruciform swimming pool fed with water from a thermal spring.

Today Addis Ababa is the unchallenged diplomatic capital of Africa. More than seventy embassies, and consular representatives cluster in the mountain city where the Organization of African Unity and the UN Economic Commission for Africa have their headquarters.

With a population of around three million, Addis Ababa is located at the centre of Shoa region, around which lie all of the country's other administrative districts. Thus, geographically, it stands at the very heart of Ethiopia. The grain-producing areas lie to the north, north-west and east of the city while the green gold (coffee) areas lie to the west and south. The capital enjoys excellent connections with all of Ethiopia's economic zones.

It was with good reason that the historian Conti-Rossini characterised Ethiopia as a rich cultural mosaic — for, in the country as a whole, there are more than eighty languages and dialects and as many cultural variations. Each one of the ethnic groups is represented somewhere in the capital. In addition, the population now also includes a large number of foreign residents from all parts of the world who contribute to the city's cosmopolitan atmosphere. The national language, Amharic, with its unique alphabet, is widely spoken throughout the country and is predominant in Addis Ababa. The principal foreign languages are English, French, Italian and Arabic.

2. City of the Hills

The appearance and character of Addis Ababa owe much to the fact that the city evolved rapidly out of what was originally a military camp on the slopes of the Entoto mountains. The visitor seeking orientation in the now extensive metropolis should realise that it sprawls over a wide stretch of land descending from the Entoto heights in the north to much lower, flatter country in the south. The slopes of the Entoto are also trisected by streams or torrent beds and these valleys serve to divide Addis Ababa into its three main sections.

To the east of Addis lies what may be termed the governmental and educational sector where one finds the following, laid out roughly north to south: the University, in several distinct campi (the main one containing the fine Ethnographic Museum of the Institute of Ethiopian Studies); the National Museum, with its notable historical and archaeological collection; the Menelik School, the country's first modern educational establishment; the first State printing-press; the Ministry of Education; the Selassie (Trinity) Cathedral, where many of the patriots of the 1936-41 war are buried; the old Menelik Palace with the adjacent Menelik Mausoleum; the Mapping Authority, where numerous maps of the country may be obtained; the Ministry of Foreign Affairs, with the Hilton Hotel opposite; the National Palace; the Filwoha thermal baths — well worth a visit; the Ghion Hotel; and the city's main square with the offices of the Ethiopian Tourism Commission facing it.

The central sector, devoted largely to commerce but in part also to government business, runs from Saint George's Cathedral and the City Hall and television studio in the north, by way of Churchill Road, to the railway station in the south.

This sector houses the headquarters of the National and Commercial Banks; the main town sales office of Ethiopian Airlines; the Post, Telephone and Telegraph office; the principal hospital (called *Tikur Anbessa*, Black Lion); the National Theatre; several cinemas; the football stadium; and two shopping centres — one, in the north, on a road running eastwards towards the University, and the other, in the south, between the Airlines' office and the railway station.

The western sector, also much involved in trade, is the site of the Mercato, Addis Ababa's principal market, as well as the city's main mosque, and of many shops rarely frequented by foreign visitors. The south-west sector of the city, which developed later than the centre, is partly residential and partly industrial. It also houses an art museum in which paintings by modern Ethiopia's premier artist, Afewerk Tekle, are often displayed.

The fact that the metropolis developed out of a military camp has had significant consequences. One is that the city is essentially scattered — for different quarters grew up initially around the separate camps of Emperor Menelik and his various lords. Another result is that the houses of the rich, constructed perhaps for those lords or their heirs, and those of the poor, some of them maybe the descendants of the nobles' servants and camp followers, are often close to each other, though of course uniform zones of housing have also come into existence, particularly in more recent years.

Several older embassies, dating back to Menelik's day, including the Italian, British, French, Russian and German, lie on the north-eastern periphery of the city while those of countries more recently accredited to Ethiopia, including some of the newly-independent African states, stand on other roads

— notably those leading to the new and old airports, to the south-east and south-west respectively.

Happily the majority of Addis Ababa's principal thoroughfares take the form of wide, two- or four-lane avenues, with trees on either side and grass reservations in the centre. Many tourist attractions and important offices are found along the capital's five main roads.

Belay Zeleke Road runs from St George's Cathedral to the foot of the eucalyptus forest in Gojjam region, passing through the city boundary — a good place for panoramic views. It was named after one of the leaders of the patriots who brought an end to the Italian occupation.

Adwa Avenue extends from just south of the City Council offices, through the busy shopping district of Piazza, to Arat Kilo. It is spanned by the Ras Makonnen Bridge and named in commemoration of the Battle of Adwa.

Development of Through Cooperation Road was named after a rural development campaign which involved 60,000 students and teachers. It runs from Jan Meda (Great Field) at Entoto to the city's main square. It also offers fine views of the city.

Asmara Road starts at the main square and extends to the city's gate to join with the old Asmara Road. It is the site of fashionable houses, many embassies and a number of new residential estates. Africa Avenue runs from Bole International Airport to the main square.

Located in Addis Ababa's western sector is the fascinating and colourful Mercato. One of the largest open-air markets in the world, it operates throughout the week and pretty much around the clock. Saturday morning, however, is its busiest period — attracting around 50,000 buyers and sellers, hailing

both from the city and from the surrounding countryside. Produce from rural areas is sold from large warehouses: vegetables, *teff,* wheat and other grains dominate.

The best way for the tourist to get to Mercato, which covers a large (and at times bewildering) area, is to hail one of the blue and white taxis which travel through the centre of the market enabling the passenger to get off when they see something of interest.

The market complex begins with small shops containing all the practical necessities of everyday life. Music screams at you from the electronics retailers who make a point of turning their radios and cassette players up to full volume to demonstrate the high decibel quality of the equipment.

Small boys wander around with goats slung over their shoulders and donkeys patiently carry loads many times their weight. The outdoor market is organised chaos. The City Council is responsible for the overall administration as the market is sited on council land; but on Saturday morning everybody does their own thing: sellers of tomatoes, cabbages, beetroot, cauliflower, carrots and an endless variety of spices, including *berbere* or chilli pepper with its unmistakable odour, sit where they can next to their wares which they guard as if they were gold.

Piles of clothes — new garments, hand-me-downs, bright red dresses and more conservative attire — are placed on top of one another making it almost impossible to discover what there is without rummaging through the whole pile. Chickens and goats wander around, seemingly oblivious to their fate, and many goats are marked with red, purple or green paint, to distinguish their ownership. Numerous corrugated iron 'shanty shops' display bright gumboots next to holy pictures,

Above: Vendor in Mercato market, one of the largest open-air markets in the world, operating throughout the week and almost round the clock.

Opposite top: Fruit stall in the Mercato, Addis Ababa's principal market.
Opposite: Broom and basket making in the Mercato.

with an enormous variety of pots, pans, dishes and plastic bowls. Children are everywhere: holding on to their parents, offering to shine shoes, selling sweets, chewing-gum or pots, or standing next to a rusting pair of scales which can tell your weight (with varying degrees of accuracy) for five or ten cents.

The Adarash market halls are divided into two sections: one specialises in imported goods (mainly clothing from Europe, Japan, India and Taiwan); the other in crafts and traditional products. Locally-made shoes are of a particularly high quality, leather being one of the country's main exports. The Adarash is also the place to go for leather bags. Most of the shops in the halls are very full — clothes hang on top of more clothes and are certainly not displayed to their best advantage. Tourists, however, may be especially interested in the good selection of scarves and brightly coloured Indian sandals.

The crafts section has more goat-skin and animal products than the downtown shops. Of particular interest are the traditional goat-skin food-carrying 'baskets', shields, horse-hair brushes and ox-horn products including a fish with a light bulb in its mouth: it may have its limitations as a lamp, but no one can question the skill and creativity which went into its design and production.

There is an endless supply of Coptic crosses, especially the elaborate Lalibela crosses. Leather paintings, pots, multi-coloured baskets and olivewood ware also abound.

Among the more unusual items offered are hippopotamus-hide shields, traditional knives, spears, prayer sticks, fur rugs, traditional musical instruments and paintings depicting the story of Solomon and the Queen of Sheba. But there are also modern shops like the Tana Complex department store — with five shopping units. Local and imported produce may be found there, including goods from the Ethiopian Household and Office Furniture company (ETHOF) and such items as photocopiers, electronic typewriters, cameras, western-style clothes, stationery and kitchenware.

In general, when shopping in the Mercato, remember that the hard-sell mentality dominates and that the first price you are offered is probably at least double that which the vendor actually hopes to be paid. Do your best to lower the price, even if it all seems an unnecessary effort for a few *birr*, but above all do not be discouraged. This is a place in which, the locals say, you can bargain for anything — even a new soul! It takes some practice to be able to compete with the experts in such an art.

After the bustle of the Mercato, a refreshing contrast — and better quality goods (particularly where gold and silver jewellery are concerned) — is offered by the city's second main shopping area, Piazza.

As its name suggests, Piazza is a legacy of the Italian occupation and still has a pronouncedly Italian character. Sprawling out along Adwa Avenue to the east of the City Council offices, it is an area of gold and silversmiths, cake shops filled with delicious pastries and doughnuts, coffee-bars specialising in frothy *capuccino*, good quality Ethiopian leather shoes, video libraries, bespoke tailors, and all manner of electronics retailers.

Meanwhile, a short distance to the west and south of Piazza, lies the long thoroughfare of Churchill Road where there is a wide variety of shops specialising in Ethiopian handicrafts and other curios and souvenirs of interest to the tourist.

Although young, Addis Ababa is a repository of many historical artefacts and the centre of Ethiopia's cultural life.

Above: Piazza, an interesting area of Addis Ababa, its name a legacy of Italian occupation.

Previous page top: Music shop in Piazza, den of mind-blowing sound.
Previous page below: "Aden Pastry" in Piazza, pastries, doughnuts, cakes,
capuccino and a place to sit down.

Fittingly, the visitor will find a good range of museums there which give insight into many different aspects of the country's rich heritage of civilisation.

An interesting overview of crafts, culture and art, for example, is provided by the Institute of Ethiopian Studies Ethnological Museum, housed in the university complex. Its showcases are filled with costumes, textiles, ornaments, pottery, horn and ivory work, leather work, basketry, gourds and tobacco pipes, cowrie-shell decorations, ironwork, woodwork and furniture and riding equipment. Information about the country's many distinct ethnic groups abounds and makes an absorbing subject of study.

The Museum is divided into two main sections: the ethnological section, containing the physical artefacts of centuries of agricultural life, and the arts section, which contains a cross-section of authentic painting organised into themes.

The ethnological section is arranged into handicrafts areas. There are different patterns and types of clothing, corresponding to the different ethnological regions — Tigray, Harar, Jimma, Gondar, or Shoa. There is everyday clothing, warrior dress, festival and religious clothing. The looms and spinning mechanisms are also displayed, as well as some examples of jewellery and adornments. There are sections displaying tools and utensils, saddles and bits, boats and ploughs.

In the arts section, one can see paintings reflecting the hunting and farming cultures of Ethiopia, folk legends, religion and war. There are fine illuminated manuscripts from Ethiopia's ancient Christian tradition, as well as paintings chronicling the battle of Adwa (1896) and the demise of the Italians in 1941. The style of painting is largely static over the centuries, in marked contrast to the sort of modern art now being produced by Ethiopia's artists.

Elsewhere the National Archaeological Museum conveys the passage of time in the way that the Ethnological Museum conveys its detail. The exhibits start with the earliest inhabitants of Ethiopia, from wild animals to the 3.5 million-year-old skeleton of Lucy, mankind's oldest-known progenitor, found at Hadar in the Ethiopian section of the Great Rift Valley. Following this are explanations of the country's pre-Axumite culture, and the riches of the Axumites themselves, with a combination of photographic and archaeological material as illustration. Next the medieval empire of Gondar is described, with photographs of the castles and palaces there, and the story is continued to cover the post-Gondarene period up to the era of the great modernisers, Tewodros and Menelik. Upstairs there are stunning examples of traditional aristocratic ceremonial dress, robes and crowns, and an enormous decorated throne. There is also a selection of modern art and culture, including work by Afewerk Tekle who has created, among other things, a large stained-glass design in Africa Hall, Headquarters of the UN Economic Commission for Africa.

Opened in November 1986, the Addis Ababa Museum is the city's most recent museum. Its focus is on the political, cultural and architectural history of the capital. Thus, there are photographs of the first settlements in Addis Ababa, the first eucalyptus trees, and the first cars, juxtaposed with modern views of the city showing the broad streets and high-rise blocks. The inauguration of the first school, telephone and currency are illustrated while upstairs there are examples of recent artistic work.

Above: Explorations into the goldsmiths' and silversmiths' shops of Addis Ababa are rarely disappointing, with gifts to suit all tastes and pockets.

Opposite top: Pottery and ceramics at Qetchene.
Opposite: The colourful crafts of Ethiopia.

71

The building in which the Addis Ababa Museum is housed was the home of Ras Biru Abtegebriel, Minister of War for Menelik II. It was once rented out but in 1986 craftsmen restored its former glory to house the exhibits which deal with all aspects of Addis Ababa's life from the city's founding.

It is hoped that the museum will help make future generations aware of their cultural heritage, but exhibits are not confined to items of historical interest. The museum also keeps residents up-to-date with current developments in the capital and one section focuses on the future.

The National Postal Museum, which has a complete set of all the stamps ever printed in Ethiopia, is a philatelist's paradise. The stamps, mounted on album pages, are clearly labelled in Amharic and English. The collection starts with the first Menelik issue of 1894 following the imperial edict of that year which established the Ethiopian Postal Administration. Ethiopian stamps were valid for internal use only until Ethiopia joined the Universal Postal Union on 1 November 1908. Some stamps printed before the Italian occupation were withheld from circulation until the time of liberation and embellished with a large red V.

The museum, established in 1975, also has many of the original drawings, approved designs, examples of the printers' art, printers' proofs and other items unique to Ethiopian philately. Stamp design competitions are held for new issues. Many Ethiopian stamps have won medals at international competitions.

The Ethiopian collection is permanent, but the museum also houses displays of stamps from other Universal Postal Union members, ranging from El Salvador to New Zealand, which are changed every six months. The Philatelic Section of the

Post Office sells first-day covers and publishes pamphlets about new stamp issues.

For those visitors with a specialist interest in rare books, or with legitimate research interests, the National Library, with its collection of more than 100,000 volumes, contains the most comprehensive collection of Ethiopian literature in the country. Established just after the end of the Italian occupation, the library was reorganised into four divisions in 1975.

The National Library Division is responsible for the development of library services throughout the country. Its Ethiopian collection consists of manuscripts, rare books, limited editions and fine bindings, ancient maps and engravings and books relating to Ethiopia published abroad — 20,000 books and manuscripts in total. Among the most valuable are the four Gospels, an early fourteenth-century illuminated manuscript — probably the oldest still-surviving in the country — the Pauline Epistles, a fifteenth-century manuscript found at the monastery of Lake Haiq in Wollo region, and services for Passion Week originally belonging to the monastery of Bizen in northern Ethiopia.

Other interesting manuscripts include an Old and New Testament Bible. It took five calligraphers five years and 500 sheepskins to produce this. A silver-plated prayer book belonging to a member of the royal family, and the first book published in Amharic abroad are in the collection.

Elderly gentlemen in charge of the ancient scripts, which are locked in a safe that would be the envy of any bank, painstakingly copy and restore old manuscripts in danger of deterioration.

The legal deposit department of the National Library

acquires three copies of all new publications printed in Ethiopia — even before the publishers have delivered the material to the clients or bookshops. A National Bibliography and National Periodicals Index records the number of titles published in the country every year.

The National Archives Division advises government departments and other organisations on the best way to store obsolete documents until they can be accommodated in the National Library, for which a new building is planned.

The public library service contains a comprehensive collection of general and reference and specialist books on a variety of topics including political ideology, social sciences, literature in Amharic, and so forth. It boasts 600 readers a day, mainly students.

When the new building is complete the National Library, which is open only to researchers from *bona fide* institutions, will focus on the housing of national documents and books on Ethiopia published both within the country and abroad.

The biggest and most modern student library in Ethiopia is the Addis Ababa University Library which boasts half a million volumes. The library system consists of the J.F. Kennedy Library on the main campus and branch libraries such as the Science Library, the Technical Library, the Medical Library, the Law Library and the country's principal research library, the Library of the Institute of Ethiopian Studies.

Addis Ababa also has much of interest to offer the theatre-goer. The City Hall Theatre, for example, seats an audience of 1,000 and is usually filled to capacity because of the high quality of the performances staged there. Elsewhere, the 1,400-seat National Theatre, established in the 1940s, focuses on the promotion of drama (local and foreign), modern and folk

dancing and popular and serious music. It also screens films, but this function is gradually being phased out.

Every Thursday between 1600 and 1800 hours, a special cultural programme crams into two hours: folk dancing, modern dance and jazz, a short drama, poetry reading and acrobatics. Revival theatre — the bringing back of past dramas — has also been introduced.

Every possible space is used. Some dressing rooms spill out into the corridor. However a comprehensive refurbishing programme was underway in 1993.

The reception hall on the ground floor, with a coffee bar frequented by everyone who is someone in the capital's cultural world, is used for banquets, weddings and orchestras, and a theatre restaurant is also planned.

The international outdoor stadium is the focal point for sport in Addis Ababa. It was built in 1968 for 27,000 spectators. In addition to all the usual sports facilities, medical services and a sauna are available at the stadium.

Football is very popular, with many important matches taking place at the stadium where Ethiopia won the third Africa Cup, and where the sixth and tenth Africa Cup finals were also staged. Athletics is also popular, and Ethiopia excels at producing long-distance and marathon runners who benefit from training at high altitude. Teams are often taken outside Addis Ababa to even higher ground for their workouts.

A new gymnasium opened at Arat Kilo in January 1987. Facilities for canoeing, archery (at Jan Meda) and shooting (twenty-five kilometres out of Addis Ababa) are also being developed.

There is a bowling alley at Emboy Mesk — a recreational centre which also has a restaurant and a children's playground

Above: Municipality, Town Hall and Addis Ababa TV station.

Above: Attractive circular Commercial Bank of Ethiopia

in a pleasant garden setting off the Debre Zeit Road. The Guenet Hotel also has excellent bowling facilities. There is a horse racing club at Jan Meda and an equestrian club situated near the Victory Department Store.

For those interested in swimming, whether for pleasure or fitness, the Ghion Hotel has an Olympic-standard swimming pool and there is a cruciform, thermally-heated pool at the Hilton. Bathing in natural hot mineral springs is possible at the Filwoha Baths. There are tennis courts at the Ghion, Hilton, Guenet and Taitu Hotels.

There are a number of excellent international restaurants in Addis Ababa where Swiss, Italian, Indian, Chinese and Middle Eastern menus are served, and also a range of establishments specialising in traditional Ethiopian food. A review follows of restaurants as independent establishments and of the restaurants in the main hotels.

The Cottage Restaurant, as its name suggests, resembles a Swiss cottage. It has not been obstructed by large buildings and stands near a large overgrown paddock close to the Harambee Hotel. Behind it is a river, and on one side a long garden whose prize-winning roses grace the tables.

The original proprietor, a Mr Dentman from Switzerland, imported the furniture, including ashtrays and condiments sets. The Ethiopian proprietors who took over the business when he returned to Switzerland are trying to retain the original decor. Only candle-light and the occasional electric lamp are used for illumination. The carpets and tablecloths are bright red and complement the dark brown wooden furniture.

A variety of Swiss and continental dishes are served, including tempting ice-creams with fruit salad or baked bananas.

80

At the back of the restaurant is a popular English-style pub where customers who lost games of darts have left their ties.

Castelli's, still run by the proprietor who established it almost forty years ago, specialises in Italian food. A house speciality, spaghetti in gorgonzola sauce, is particularly recommended. Meanwhile for those seeking a less gourmet-style Italian meal, the **Oroscope Pizzeria**, off Churchill Road, serves steak and a variety of other dishes in addition to its pizzas.

Blue Tops, on King George Street, above Arat Kilo, is a welcome addition to Addis Ababa's selection of international restaurants. Two pyramid-shaped tented enclosures cover the main dining areas. One of these is open only at lunchtimes and specialises in quick snacks, such as hamburgers and a delicious variety of drinks and ice-creams. The other is a dinner restaurant which features, grills, pastas and a range of vegetarian specialities.

Petit Paris, near the Old Airport, a newly opened restaurant, offers a wide range of first-class French cuisine and is well worth a visit.

The **Sangham Restaurant**, along Africa Avenue on the way to the airport, is popular with Addis Ababa's resident Asian community as well as with other foreigners and Ethiopians. Serving hot and delicious Indian meals, it specialises in curries with rice and *nan* breads.

The **China Bar**, near the entrance to the Ghion hotel, offers a menu with 101 different dishes — probably the most varied in Addis Ababa. Seafood (sometimes in short supply), poultry, pork, dumplings, noodles and Chinese-style vegetables combined in numerous ways are guaranteed to satisfy all tastes.

Above: Addis Ababa Restaurant specialises in traditional dishes.

Opposite: The popular Castelli Restaurant, Piazza.

The proprietors are convinced that their restaurant is the most decorated in Africa. Thousands of dragons play on the ceilings, the walls resemble those of a colourful Mandarin castle and Chinese lamps help create a truly Oriental atmosphere.

The spices and lychee wines are imported mainly from Taiwan, and the restaurant has a large Asian and European clientele. There is a buffet lunch between 1200 and 1300 hours on Thursday but there is no need to book as the restaurant can comfortably seat 165 people.

Another restaurant which serves a variety of Chinese dishes is the **Hong Kong**. It is located near St Saviour Cathedral behind a striking red gate with colourful designs.

Lalibela Restaurant, near the stadium, has a decor which recalls the famous Lalibela rock churches. Elaborate carvings adorn the tables, chairs and walls. A tree with bottles for leaves decorates the downstairs pub and snack bar. The upstairs restaurant, which seats seventy, is spacious. Pepper steak is the speciality and meals are served with French fries or rice. Windows close to the ceiling let in the sunlight and give a good view of the stadium — you can see athletes training. The restaurant arranges special banquets for government guests and businessmen.

The **Rendezvous** is a large round building close to the offices of the Ethiopian Tourism Commission. The speciality is steaks cooked on a large open grill in the centre of the dining area. A different cake is prepared every day and patrons can enjoy the sunshine and the flowers in numerous window-boxes on the terrace. The sparsely-decorated restaurant is a favourite meeting place for Ethiopian civil servants and businessmen during lunchhour.

The **Kokeb** restaurant is worth visiting just for the ride in the glass-windowed lift which takes you up through the trees to the tenth floor of the apartment block in which it is situated. The panoramic views of the city are spectacular at night. The display of horse-riding equipment and traditional jewellery would not shame any museum. There are saddle-like stools as well as private tables on the terrace. Patrons can watch colour television while dining. European food is available, as well as a five-dish Ethiopian meal. The ceiling of one of the terraces is lined with shields of ox-hide, bamboo twigs and climbing shrubs.

In traditional Ethiopian cuisine, meat is a staple food — and very popular. Beef is eaten cooked, dried or raw in all parts of the country. Mutton dishes supplement the diet at higher altitudes, along with goat meat, and camel is eaten in the desert lowlands. Fish, too, is popular among the people living near lakes and the coast. Nile perch, tilapia and catfish are all delicious. Red Sea fish are eaten in coastal regions.

The national dish is *injera* and *wat*. *Injera*, a very fine type of bread resembling a pancake, is made from the indigenous grain, *teff,* which comes in three qualities: the top quality is white, followed by various shades of grey. *Injera* may come rolled. Usually, however, it is spread flat on the plate and various types of *wat* are placed on top. Wat consists of approximately twenty types of spicy sauces — chicken, lamb and vegetable being the most popular. Some are served with boiled eggs. Especially interesting is the raw, finely-chopped beef (usually highly spiced), *gommen wat* (made with spinach), *beg tibs* (roast pieces of lamb), and *alicha doro wat* (a mild chicken dish). *Kotcho* is a popular pancake made of *ensete* (false banana) root which has been pounded and fermented. Along

Above: Coffee ceremony at Tyia.

Opposite: Ghion (Tukul) National Restaurant.

with the traditional Ethiopian meal one would normally drink either *tej* (a type of mead) or *tella* (beer). Also well worth trying are *araki* liqueurs made from such ingredients as honey and milk.

The capital, naturally, boasts many restaurants serving good traditional food. Amongst the best of these is the **Addis Ababa Restaurant** where not only the food is traditional. The century-old building has a long history. It was once the home of Queen Zauditu, who divorced her husband, Dejateh Wube, to marry into the royal family.

As well as its Ethiopian patrons, the restaurant has a large foreign clientele who adapt readily to the Ethiopian custom of eating without knives and forks.

Another traditional restaurant specialising in the best of Ethiopian cuisine is the **Karamara** (on Africa Avenue between Revolution Square and Bole Airport). A grouping of large, airy rondavels, the Karamara — popular with tourists and Ethiopians alike — offers an authentic atmosphere and live entertainment provided by strolling musicians who, for a fee, will *ad lib* humourous or flattering songs about yourself or members of your party.

The **Finefine Hotel**, on the road between the Harambee Hotel and the Hilton, also serves traditional food in an elegant restaurant with an impressive wooden decor. The restaurant is divided into a more intimate downstairs section with tables and chairs and an upstairs section with small leather stools and mats embroidered with a lion motif.

The Finefine, once the home of a *Ras* (nobleman) who brought in Greek craftsmen to transform the house with artistic woodwork, is signposted with the word *Adarash*, Amharic for a great hall, and stands adjacent to the Filwoha

(Hot Spring) Baths — which are excellent for stimulating the appetite.

Ethiopian dishes are also served at the Hilton Hotel (the Saturday buffet), the Ghion Hotel, the Guenet Hotel, the Ethiopia Hotel, and the Hotel d'Afrique — which has decorated its basement area to resemble a traditional Ethiopian eating house with private, curtained-off alcoves for small or large parties.

Addis Ababa has a wide variety of hotel accommodation to offer its many international guests — ranging from the cosmopolitan luxury of the Hilton at one end of the scale to cheaper but still comfortable tourist hotels like the **Blue Nile** or the **Maskal Flower** at the other.

The **Addis Ababa Hilton International** is rightly regarded as one of Africa's leading hotels — offering luxury accommodation and a comprehensive range of business and recreational facilities in the centre of the city. Situated in fifteen acres of landscaped gardens off Menelik II Avenue (opposite the Ministry of Foreign Affairs), the Hilton consists of a 261-room tower, and a 180-room garden-wing. This latter consists mainly of serviced apartments aimed at meeting the needs of long-stay guests. All rooms, whether in the extension or the tower, are connected to a closed-circuit video-TV system offering a range of in-house movies. Each room also has its own mini-bar and individual air-conditioning.

The hotel's food and beverage facilities are of the high standard that Hilton guests worldwide have come to expect. The two principal restaurants are the prestigious **Harar Grill**, which serves a fine selection of French *cordon bleu* food, and — in the Garden Wing — the Mexican-Italian **Jacaranda Restaurant**. In addition there is a pizzeria, and a coffee-shop,

Above: Hilton Hotel tennis courts.

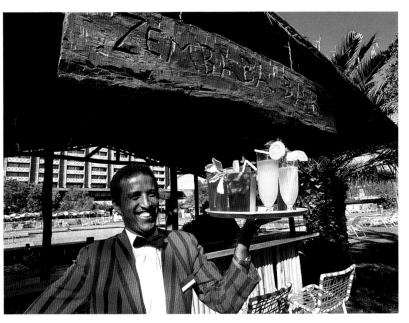

Above: "Zembaba Bar" with cocktail waiter at the Hilton Hotel.

known as the **Kaffa House**, which provides a full but quick meal service throughout the day (including breakfast) and a traditional Ethiopian hot buffet on Saturdays.

Outdoors, the **Gazebo Club** offers a range of snacks and barbecues in a setting that overlooks the Hilton's famous swimming pool which is filled with warm mineral water from a deep thermal spring.

Designed in a cruciform shape echoing the architecture of Saint George's church at Lalibela, the pool is surrounded by pleasant gardens offering an ideal venue for postprandial sunbathing and relaxation. Meanwhile, for those of a more energetic disposition, the hotel's floodlit tennis courts are just a few seconds walk away, while jacuzzi, sauna and professional massage services are also available.

Other facilities within the hotel include a pharmacy and bookshop, a well-stocked duty-free shop, and a souvenir shop. Ethiopian Airlines and the National Tour Operation also have sales offices in the hotel's spacious lobby.

The **Ghion**, Addis Ababa's second hotel in terms of luxury and services, is situated in extensive private gardens close to the city's main square. Run by the government's National Hotels Corporation, it consists of a central building with 103 rooms surrounded by bungalows and apartments offering a further ninety-seven rooms — respectively the Ghion Bungalows (studio bedrooms and junior suites); the Demera Suites (made up of six blocks, each containing two suites and two singles); and the Riviera Suites (offering spacious accommodation, each with a bedsitting room, a spare bedroom and a kitchenette).

Particularly noted for its extensive and beautiful gardens (boasting more than forty different species of flowering plants), the Ghion was completely redecorated and renovated in 1983 and has been well-maintained ever since. The bright and spacious lobby leads past the National Tour Operation sales office, and souvenir shop into a comfortable lounge bar, ideal for pre-dinner drinks. Upstairs, the elegant main restaurant seats 200 people and beyond this is the **Tukul**, a snack bar which has also built up a reputation for catering small banquets and private functions. Additional food-and-beverage outlets include a breakfast room off the main restaurant, and **Unity House** which stands in the gardens to the front of the hotel.

In the gardens to the rear of the hotel is the Ghion's Olympic-standard swimming pool. There the **pool bar** offers a complete snack service — including barbecues and pizzas, and specialises in draft beer.

The Ghion also boasts Addis Ababa's only **casino**. This provides the full range of games of chance — including *chemin de fer*, blackjack and, of course, roulette. A further small dining room is situated within the casino.

Like the Ghion, three other city hotels — the **Wabe Shebelle**, the **Ethiopia** and the **Hotel d'Afrique** — have also recently been renovated and are now beautifully furnished and decorated. The Ethiopia offers an exceptionally high standard of accommodation in the heart of Addis Ababa's business and commercial district, only a few minutes walk from the National Theatre and the headquarters of the National Bank of Ethiopia. The hotel fronts onto a pleasant street, the central island of which is lined with elegant palm trees. Guests enjoy this view from the terrace, where a full bar service is available. The Wabe Shebelle boasts bright and airy rooms with comfortable beds and attractive pastel decor. The

Above: Side of the oldest hotel in Addis Ababa - Taytu Hotel.

Above: Traditional Ethiopian dancers.

Hotel d'Afrique offers a high standard of accommodation at very competitive prices. All the rooms are beautifully furnished and decorated while the suites offer the additional attraction of balcony views over the city of Addis Ababa.

The **Ras Hotel**, on Churchill Road close to the Railway Station, is something of an Addis Ababa tradition, being one of the oldest hotels in the young city. Its ground-floor bar, to the right of the lobby, is a popular and cosmopolitan meeting place, where you can enjoy the authentic Addis Ababa atmosphere while sampling good food, capuccino or, perhaps, a cold beer. Upstairs on the second floor is a much larger and more formal restaurant (capacity about 200) with an adjoining breakfast room. This restaurant is recommended for its Saturday buffet. Late on Friday and Saturday evenings it is transformed into a swinging nightclub with live bands performing.

The **Harambee Hotel** is centrally located close to the Ethiopia Hotel and the National Bank headquarters. It offers reasonably-priced accommodation and a pleasant ambience. Its lobby boasts an extremely well-stocked souvenir shop with a wide range of amber and silver jewellery, crosses and embroidery. Upstairs on the first floor is the Magala Lounge, imaginatively decorated in the style of the traditional homes of the ancient Muslim city of Harar. Its whitewashed walls are hung with basketwork and other handicrafts, while its low lattice ceiling and its cosy individual booths add to the atmosphere. Through from the Magala Lounge, but continuing in the same style of decor, is the **Harar Restaurant** which seats eighty people in intimate comfort and serves a high-standard international menu.

For those interested in a self-catering holiday the **National**

Hotel, converted from a seven-storey apartment block, has cooking facilities on each floor. It is conveniently located on Menelik II Avenue opposite Africa Hall.

The **Blue Nile** is the most basic of the government hotels, and is not generally recommended for tourists. Those wanting a small cheap hotel would do better to try the **Maskel Flower** on the Debre Zeit road, the **Tourist Hotel** at Arat Kilo near the university, or the country's oldest hotel, the **Taytu**, formerly the Etegé, which was established during the time of Menelik II.

Service in government hotels is friendly and polite but sometimes a little slow. Staff are generally willing to go out of their way to help tourists with taxi bookings and other practical day-to-day matters.

The international atmosphere and temperate climate make Addis Ababa a particularly good centre for businessmen. Daily flights connect the capital directly with Europe, the Middle East, Asia, and the rest of Africa, and through quick connections in Europe, with America.

Communications are excellent. Telephone, telex and cable lines reach out all over the world, and the mail service is swift and reliable.

There is a rail connection with Djibouti at the entrance to the Red Sea, good international roads, a public transport system and plenty of taxis to ensure the businessman never misses an appointment.

Addis Ababa, is a fast-growing cosmopolitan city. Each year it welcomes increasing numbers of businessmen and travellers from all parts of the world. It is also the meeting place for the economic and political minds of the African continent. Experts in many fields make frequent stops in the tree-crowded city,

Above: Aerial view of Addis.

Opposite: Section of Ethiopian artist Afewerk Tekle's stained glass window in Africa Hall, Addis.

home of the Organization of African Unity and the United Nations Economic Commission for Africa.

Important groups in addition to the OAU and the ECA also have their regional headquarters there. They include the United Nations Development Programme, UNICEF, UNHCR, FAO, UNESCO, and UNCTAD, as well as the ILO, ICO, ITU, the World Meteorological Organization and the International Bank for Reconstruction and Development (World Bank).

Africa Hall hosts thousands of conferences, the most common being meetings on African Trade and Industrial Promotions, Economic Co-operation, Inventory, Planning and Management. The Hall, headquarters of the UN Economic Commission for Africa, was designed by two Italian architects, Fenano and Mezzedini. Its walls are decorated with murals on glass by Ethiopia's master-artist Afewerk Tekle.

3. Addis — Street by Street

Addis Ababa is a big, sprawling, hospitable city. For most visitors an easy point of reference from which to take their bearings is Africa Hall on Menelik II Avenue. This imposing building is the headquarters of the UN Economic Commission for Africa and hosts many international conferences. It was the venue for the first meeting of the African Heads of State, at which the Organization of African Unity was formed in 1963. Many decisions important to the future of Africa have subsequently been made within these walls and it is a good starting point for a circuit tour, roughly in a clockwise direction, which covers some of Addis Ababa's most interesting aspects.

Just a few hundred metres west of Africa Hall are the Filwoha Thermal Springs, which prompted Queen Taytu to persuade her husband, Emperor Menelik II, to establish his new capital in Addis Ababa. These springs are now the site of sixteen bathing complexes, with 190 bathing cubicles and a staff of 200. On average 2,000 people come to bathe on a typical Saturday or Sunday. Sauna, physiotherapy and exercise rooms are available and the attractions of the complex include not only the curative mineral waters but also the excellent traditional restaurant in the Finefine Hotel itself where the visitor may enjoy a fabulous range of traditional *injera* and *wat* stews.

Next to Africa Hall a modern Ethiopian Orthodox church, Saint Stephanos, is worth visiting. Surrounded by beautiful gardens, it stands on the eastern flank of Addis Ababa's main square, overlooked by the offices of the Ethiopian Tourism Commission. At one end of this square is the house of a former nobleman which has been converted into the Addis Ababa Museum, made possible largely by generous donations

Opposite: St Stephanos Ethiopian Orthodox Church, adjacent to Africa Hall.

Below: Tiglachin Monument.

of artefacts from the public, and inaugurated in 1986 on the city's hundredth anniversary.

Nearby is the capital's sports stadium. Built in 1968, this 27,000-capacity arena where Ethiopia won the third Africa soccer cup also stages athletics, cycling and boxing as well as pop concerts and cultural festivals. It is flanked on its southern side by Makonnen Avenue which leads on to Mexico Square, passing the 1929 Railway Station, built twelve years after the line from Djibouti reached Addis Ababa.

From the station's crowded entrance, the visitor looks along the impressive, rising sweep of Churchill Road which stretches into the distance towards the dominant shape of City Hall at the northern end. Characterised by the hustle and bustle of modern city life, the road passes the historic Ras Hotel in a district crowded with souvenir shops — all well worth visiting. Many hawkers work there, offering passers-by goods of variable quality: jewellery, books and silver Maria Theresa dollars, for example. Stop and look, but never feel obliged to buy. Always bargain if you find something you want.

The next point of interest, close to the Ethiopia Hotel, is the National Theatre, watched over by a towering lion built from black stone. The theatre presents a wide variety of shows with a focus on serious entertainment and cultural presentations.

Just across the road from the Ethiopia Hotel is the Ambassador, one of Addis Ababa's largest commercial cinemas. It seats 1,600 and screens an eclectic selection of films. Nearby a magnificent flower-shaped edifice houses the Commercial and National Banks of Ethiopia, and the Mortgage Company of Ethiopia.

A few-hundred metres to the north stands a monument built to commemorate those who fell in the 1977/78 war against Somalia while, across the road from the monument, is the Postal Museum. From stamps, the first of which appeared in Ethiopia in 1894, you can move on to books — some dating back to the fourteenth century — at the nearby National Library.

Slightly further off towards the Wabe Shebelle Hotel is the Hasida — Handicrafts and Small-Scale Industries Development Agency. Well worth a visit, it has a small emporium where products and tools are exhibited and crafts shops where some museum items are on sale.

The floor-plan of City Hall, which overlooks all this from the top of Churchill Road, resembles a three-cornered star in which the Council Chambers, staff offices, and a reception area used for banquets, are accommodated. There is also a theatre and an art gallery and everyone of importance in Addis Ababa's art world frequents the coffee bar.

Many of the Council's 4,000 workers mingle there over refreshments with actors, musicians and television personalities. It is also a favoured location for staging wedding receptions, particularly during the hectic weeks after Christmas and before Easter, the most popular season of the year for marriages in Ethiopia. Atop the clock tower, which draws its inspiration from Axumite architecture, a vigilant eagle watches over this section of Addis Ababa and the nearby shopping district known as the Piazza where there are a number of fashionable shops — notably those retailing high-quality gold and silver jewellery.

Immediately north of City Hall, on a roundabout at the centre of Menelik II Square, stands a statue of Menelik himself astride his favourite horse. The Italians, eager to forget their humiliating defeat at his hands at the Battle of Adwa, hid the

Opposite: The towering Lion of Judah, carved from black stone, near the National Theatre.

Left and below: Yekatit 12 Monument, and detail.

107

statue when they occupied Addis Ababa. In 1941, when they were ousted by the patriots and Allied forces, the statue of Menelik was restored to its proper place.

Nearby, slightly further to the north-west, stands Saint George's Cathedral — built by Menelik to commemorate his historic victory at Adwa. Octagonal in shape, the cathedral bears an ornate cross upon its large dome. Inside there is a feast of decorations. The best-known paintings are those by Maitre-Artiste Afewerk Tekle, who also contributed the tile murals at the top of all four walls. Other paintings include those of the Virgin Mary, the Crucifixion and scenes from the life of Saint George.

West of Menelik II Square is Abuna Petros Square, dedicated to one of the key figures in the struggle against the Italian invaders. Then Patriarch of the Ethiopian Orthodox Church, he was captured by the Italians who hoped to persuade him to uphold their rule. When he refused he was shot.

Meanwhile, to the east, at Siddist Kilo, stands another large memorial. Named Yekatit 12 it commemorates the actions of the two Ethiopians who hurled a hand grenade at Graziani, the Italian governor, who was reading a proclamation from Mussolini. The story is told in a stone carving in the shape of a book, while the subsequent reprisal atrocities are also commemorated in stone. The attempt on Graziani's life took place on 19 February 1937 — Yekatit 12 in the Ethiopian calendar.

To the north of this monument stands Addis Ababa University campus, its impressive modern buildings set in pleasant, well-landscaped gardens. The Ethnological Museum is located on campus.

Above the campus rise the southern slopes of Mount Entoto, the extensive mountain range north of Addis Ababa. There you can see two churches and the original site of Menelik's capital at Entoto — which he left to found Addis Ababa. It's a beautiful hike up the mountain. For most people, however, the altitude and the distance make a car a necessity. You may want to take a picnic lunch and enjoy a peaceful day on the forested slopes enjoying the panoramic views.

Little now remains of the early capital but high on the hill stands the church of Entoto Maryam where Menelik was crowned in 1889. It is octagonal in shape with three concentric chambers inside. These are richly decorated with Ethiopian paintings. Nearby, a museum — opened in 1986 — contains many interesting exhibits and artefacts.

Along the road past the church, at the top of the Entoto plateau, you look northwards across the farmland that stretches towards the Blue Nile Gorge, and you can visit a second church, two-storeyed Entoto Raguel, which stood at the centre of the old capital of Entoto. Stunning views expand as you climb through the eucalyptus forest to the top of Entoto.

To the south, the peak of Mount Zuquala, an extinct volcano, dominates the horizon, with Mounts Erer, Wuchacha and Manegesha in attendance, Below, in the valley, Addis Ababa spreads out amidst a canopy of green — living up in every sense to its name New Flower. At night, when viewed from this vantage point, the capital seems to be a tangled web of fairy lights.

Back in the city, close by Yekatit 12 Square, the Lion Park with its verdant gardens is a pleasant place for a well-earned coffee-break. More than a dozen lions are kept there, with

Above: Trinity Cathedral built 1935-42.

Opposite top: Stained glass window depicting Adam and Eve in Trinity Church.
Opposite: Decorated ceiling in Trinity Cathedral.

adults and cubs separated from the public by sturdy cages surrounded by a wooden fence.

Just a short stroll from the park is the National Archaeological Museum. And southwards from there, at Arat Kilo, is the Megabit 28 monument which commemorates the day when the Patriots entered Addis Ababa and liberated it — 28 April 1941. The monument takes the form of a tall obelisk surmounted by the lion of Judah, which itself stands on top of a clock with its hands fixed at 11 — the hour of liberation.

Nearby, Trinity Cathedral, built in 1941, is one of the most elegant and elaborately-decorated places of worship in the city. Particularly notable are statues of the Wise Men and of the Four Apostles.

Another point of interest in this sector of Addis Ababa is the Menelik Mausoleum, built by the Emperor's daughter Queen Zauditu to the east of the old Menelik palace. The grey stone building, topped by a large dome, commands a lovely view of the city.

Running southwards from the Menelik Palace to Addis Ababa's main square, Menelik II Avenue is undoubtedly one of the capital's most graceful thoroughfares. The formal gardens of the Hilton Hotel, the Jubilee Palace, and Africa Hall add to its tree-lined atmosphere of somnolent greenery.

4. Excursions from Addis Ababa

Located in the geographic centre of Ethiopia, Addis Ababa is ideally situated for excursions to all parts of this remarkable and beautiful country. Excellent roads, and efficient internal air connections provided by Ethiopian Airlines, mean that it is possible for even the short-stay visitor to see at least some of the main places of interest. For specific tour information the visitor is advised to contact the National Tour Operation in Addis Ababa.

South-west of Addis Ababa a good road leads to some of the loveliest scenery and places in all of Ethiopia — in that dramatic natural phenomenon, the Great Rift Valley.

You pass first through the capital's industrial sector south of the city where you can pause to stroll through an unlikely Eden for such a location — the Berhe Tsige tropical gardens, which boast more than 6,000 different varieties of endemic and exotic flora planted over several hectares.

From there the journey continues through villages and farmlands dotted with *tukuls* (traditional thatched huts) until, after an hour or so, you arrive at Debre Zeit, a busy commercial centre.

Some fifty kilometres from Addis Ababa, Debre Zeit, always colourful with bougainvillea, flame trees and jacarandas (which envelop it in a fragrant canopy of reds, purples and oranges) is encircled by five of the crater lakes which distinguish the African Rift for much of its length.

From the terrace of the Ras Hotel, perched high on the rim of the principal crater, there's a splendid view of Lake Hora — popular for waterskiing, boating, fishing and birdwatching.

The most dramatic lake, Bishoftu, is invisible from the main road. You have to turn off, climb a small hill and there it is — its stunningly deep walls plunging almost sheer to the surface of its mysterious waters, reputed locally to be bottomless and to contain an evil spirit.

Another excursion off the main highway from Debre Zeit takes you to an almost perfect volcanic cone — Mount Zuqualla which rises 600 metres above the surrounding plain. The shallow lake inside the caldera, lined with juniper forest, is regarded as sacred. An ancient monastery stands on the crater rim looking down on the lake. Colobus monkeys leap through the lichen-draped juniper trees which are often cloaked in mist. The stiff climb to the top of the crater may take as much as three hours but is rewarded by a majestic view to the east, looking down into the Rift Valley. A vineyard stands nearby and, in season, succulent grapes are offered for sale by roadside vendors.

Back on the main highway, some kilometres beyond Debre Zeit, the road

113

Above: Profusion of purple Bougainvillea.

Opposite: Lake Babagoya near Debre Zeit.

divides into two at Mojo, a small transit town boasting a filling station and two hotels. The left fork leads towards the Awash river, some of the most interesting features of which are only a few kilometres further on at a point where the hot blue waters of thermal springs gush up from the molten interior of the Rift to merge with the silt-laden waters of the Awash. Fish leap and splash in the churning torrent, preyed on by lurking crocodiles which wait furtively in the thick undergrowth along the bank. Further downstream there is a hippo pool.

The track continues from there to the sprawling Wonji sugar estate and thence into the pleasant, bustling town of Nazareth with its fine hotels — including the excellent Adama built around a central swimming pool. One of the biggest cattle collecting points in Ethiopia, and close to lush citrus and fruit orchards, the streets of Nazareth are alive with the blossoms and the fragrance of tropical plants.

From there it is not too long a drive — two hours in all from Addis Ababa — to Sodere, a favourite weekend resort for the capital's citizens. It is a kind of spa which has developed around the volcanic mineral springs that constantly replenish its two swimming pools with clear, blue, warm water. The hotel stands on the banks of the Awash river with its thick and ancient gallery forest of giant trees casting a cool shadow over the grounds.

There is a range of accommodation within the complex: a five-star hotel, tent-like cabins, two-room bungalows on the river bank or high up on the hillside which looms above, and a camping area on the river bank.

For leisure there is swimming and the hotel grounds and, beyond them, fine walks through typical Rift Valley countryside along the river where monkeys and baboons play in the trees, hippos dive and surface, and crocodiles bask in the noon heat. Accompanying it all is the piping call of the go-away bird, the haunting cry of the fish-eagle, and the vivid spectacle of bright blue starlings and yellow weaver birds.

Beyond Sodere, 190 kilometres from the capital, you arrive at the gate of the Awash National Park with its headquarters set down near the dramatic Awash Falls — a wide, thundering cataract when the river is in spate.

One of the most beautiful spots is Kudu Valley which takes its name from the large — and rare — antelope sometimes to be seen there. There is other game, too: oryx, Soemmerring's gazelle, wild pig, the tiny dik-dik antelope, waterbuck, zebra, and cats such as leopard, cheetah and the smaller serval. You may also catch a glimpse of the elusive klipspringer, a diminutive antelope well adapted to its rocky home and a coat that absorbs

the shock of falls and strange hoofs that allow it to leap around cliffs and ledges like a mountain goat.

Another attraction is the area of hot springs on the north side of the park, lying like a great oasis surrounded by tall green doum palms amidst a dry desert of scrub and thorn trees. Emerging from several deep sources, the superheated water quickly cools to temperatures that swimmers can tolerate and spreads out in widening pools of translucent turquoise.

However, long before you reach there — at Mojo, in fact, where the road divides — the traveller has the option to turn directly into the Great Rift Valley and to head for the lakes that spread southwards like a necklace of lustrous pearls. The scenery and passing pageant of daily life create memories that linger for a lifetime.

You get the feel of the Great Rift Valley, one of the most dramatic landscapes in the world, even though the escarpment mountain walls there are more gentle than elsewhere in the country.

Almost as soon as you leave Mojo you may see the many camel trains which plod along this part of the Rift, the beasts swaying forward loaded with the charcoal that they have carried from acacia forests further south.

Soon after passing Mojo you will cross the Koka Dam which bridges the Awash at a narrow neck in its course — a development that has produced a man-made lake every bit as beautiful as those others that nature created when it forged the Great Rift Valley. You may be tempted to stay awhile and luxuriate in this sylvan setting of shady trees and cool water. Vast flocks of Egyptian geese wade in the shallows and hippo frolic among the reed beds.

Following the highway onwards past the western shore of Lake Koka and, on from there through acacia woodlands, you eventually reach Lake Zway, the northernmost of Ethiopia's seven true Rift Valley lakes. Twenty-six kilometres long and eighteen kilometres wide, Zway is also one of the largest lakes. It is dotted with several islands, the largest, Debre Tsion, containing an ancient monastery, and its shores are fringed with tall fig trees that, during years of bountiful rain, are lapped by the swollen water's edge. Marabou storks roost in the trees at sundown and others feed on the grassy stretch that flourishes along the alluvial shoreline. To the north, where the Mekli river flows in to replenish the waters of Lake Zway, there a wide bay in which hippo gather in abundance.

Between Zway and the next lake, Langano, are the ruins of an old fortress towering over the village of Adami Tulu.

117

Above: Hippo family, nature's true amphibians.

Opposite top left: Darter on Lake Chamo.
Opposite top right: Sacred ibis and egret.
Opposite: Egyptian geese.

Lake Langano itself is a favoured resort for weekenders, 215 kilometres from the capital, set against the blue-grey backdrop of the Arsi mountains. Less for the nature lover, more for the sportsman and sun worshipper, Langano provides an ideal retreat for sun-bathing, watersports, and laid-back good living with excellent fishing and fine accommodation available.

A short distance due west of Langano lies Lake Abiata — its waters a sheen of iridescent pink, a veritable carpet of flamingos floating and wading in the shallows of its blue bays. Great white pelicans soar over its alkaline waters from nearby Lake Shala, while myriad other species — amongst them fish eagles, cormorants and darters — perch in the dried branches of dead acacia trees well beyond the shoreline, creating a fantasy of silhouettes at sundown.

Lake Shala, where all of Abiata's birds breed and nest, forms a counter-balance to Langano's modern delights — a pristine wilderness that is a treasury of bird-life and landscapes, part of the Shala-Abiata National Park.

But yet more awaits the traveller. Through Wondo Guenet, beyond the town of Shahshamene, there is a lovely wooded valley of ancient, indigenous Ethiopian trees with a lodge set in gardens of cedar, palm and citrus groves overlooking the Rift Valley. There the dust and tiredness of travel are washed away in the soothing waters of the natural hot springs, just a few metres from an icy, sparkling, mountain stream.

Beyond is a lacustrine spa resort without peer — Lake Awasa. Small by comparison with those that precede and follow it, Awasa nevertheless boasts luxury hotels and a diverse range of watersports.

But for those who yearn truly to get away from it all, Lakes Abaya and Chamo, far to the south, beckon: wilderness retreats that demand more time than the average visitor may be able to afford.

Managesha, Wuchacha, Addis Alem, Ambo
Another excursion from Addis Ababa leads out on the road west. Just a few kilometres from the city, at Asko, it passes through a traditional potters village, where locally-made ceramic utensils are sold. Soon after you pass Addis Ababa's water reservoir, Gafarsa, which hosts large populations of indigenous birds and boasts an attractive Austrian restaurant which serves as a magnet for citizens during their leisure hours and is noted for its Sunday buffet lunch.

Nearby rise the peaks of two extinct volcanoes, Manegesha and Mount Wuchacha, where indigenous juniper forests cover the lower slopes. Oddly enough, the primal Managesha Forest cloaks the slopes not of its namesake but of Wuchacha. Some four centuries old, these trees rise thirty or more metres into the sky and are accessible from a winding dirt track.

In glades and clearings the shy creatures of the forest flit to and fro among the giant juniper, podocarpus, palms and kosso. Klipspringer and Menelik's bushbuck pause fearfully at each footfall to vanish like shadowy phantoms in a trice. Through the topmost branches swing glorious black-and-white Colobus monkeys and, on the forest floor, there are frequent packs of baboons. Emperor Zara Ya'qob of Shoa planted this forest in the sixteenth century.

Stop at Addis Alem for a brief visit to the strangely-decorated little church of Debre Tsion. Then on to Ambo, the source of Ethiopia's popular bottled mineral water, and beyond to the vineyards. A side trip to the waterfall on the Guder river is also worth making before lunch at the Ras Hotel in Ambo and then a swim in the hot pool — returning in the late afternoon to Addis Ababa.

Debra Libanos and the Blue Nile Gorge

Another excursion leads northwards out of Addis Ababa. The road climbs at first up the steep slopes of the Entoto escarpment, through eucalyptus groves, past the old capital and its historic churches, to emerge on the top of the plateau a few kilometres from Ethiopia's satellite ground station at Sululta. The land there reaches a high point of more than 3,000 metres — but remember that Addis Ababa itself stands at 2,500 metres and is, in fact, the world's third highest capital.

Following this road still further you are off on a day-long excursion to one of the physical wonders of this planet — the Blue Nile Gorge. Once at the top of the plateau you drive across seemingly endless tablelands where the air is crisp and cool and the fragrance of thyme and heath fill it with a bracing pungency.

Ninety minutes from Addis, at a distance of just over 100 kilometres, a turning leads down to the thirteenth-century monastery of Debra Libanos on the rim of a precipitous gorge almost a kilometre deep. A new church stands just below the old and in the cliffs above lives a solitary hermit. The new church has beautiful stained-glass windows and some marvellous mosaic figures on its facade.

Not long after Debra Libanos, less than a kilometre from the main road, a turning takes you to a curious legacy of European interest in Ethiopia — a

121

bridge that seems to have stepped straight out of a Hans Christian Andersen fairy tale. Built by the Portuguese in the sixteenth century it spans a tributary of the Blue Nile.

When the Blue Nile itself leaves Lake Tana, far to the north, it begins one of the most spectacular river journeys in the world — in the course of which it carves its way through a tremendous gorge that is both deeper and wider than America's Grand Canyon. Nothing can prepare you for the first sight of this remarkable natural phenomenon. Over a mile wide, and almost as deep, the Blue Nile Gorge suddenly appears at a bend in the road, filling the first-time visitor with breathless wonder. From there the road then winds precariously down more than a thousand metres to the bed of the gorge. This dramatic descent takes about forty-five minutes by car and seems to last a lifetime. At the bottom the Blue Nile is crossed by a modern single-span bridge. You can enjoy a picnic lunch by the river on the other side before returning to Addis Ababa early in the evening.

Bahar Dar, Lake Tana, Blue Nile Falls

Alternatively you can choose to travel on by road from the Blue Nile Gorge in the direction of Lake Tana. Perhaps a better option for the visitor who is short of time, however, is to take the daily scheduled air service from Addis Ababa (the flight takes less than an hour) and stay overnight at one of the pleasant hotels in Bahar Dar — the town which stands at the southernmost point of Lake Tana. From there you can make the journey to the Blue Nile Falls thirty kilometres downstream from the point where the river leaves the lake, approaching them on foot from a nearby village.

The name of that village is *Tissisat*, and this name, meaning water that smokes is also applied locally to the Falls themselves — which are reached after crossing a spectacular seventeenth-century Portuguese bridge and then climbing the side of a rolling hill. At the top, the falls suddenly come into view, a mist-enshrouded explosion of water crashing with thunderous roar into the gorge below. The falls draw their ceaseless energy from the vast expanse of Lake Tana, which has a surface area of 3,700 square kilometres dotted with more than thirty islands. Most of these are inhabited and some are places of religious seclusion which have long inspired mystics and men of religion. Many monasteries, some dating back as far as the fourteenth century, are located there and can be visited easily from Bahar Dar where first-class hotels on the lake's shore, and a choice of facilities and cuisine, ensure that the visitor enjoys every convenience and luxury.

Gondar

It is possible to travel on from Bahar Dar to one of the most magnificent places in Africa — Gondar, the fabled city of castles, which by road is 750 kilometres from Addis Ababa, nestling at the foot of the Simien Mountains. A regular Ethiopian Airlines service also connects the capital with Gondar, providing the quickest method of access for the visitor who wishes to see the castles and return the next day.

Standing in rolling parkland, the two-storeyed castle of King Fasilidas was the earliest of these — so impressive that a visiting Yemeni envoy, Hasan ibn Ahmed el-Haimi, thought it one of the most marvellous of buildings, designed by a master builder from India. Fasilidas' son, Yohannes I, inspired the building of another two-storeyed castle as his library, as well as a larger castle, with an imposing tower for use as his chancery.

Another edifice associated with Fasilidas is the Bathing Palace which stands at the edge of a man-made lake on the outskirts of Gondar. That lake is normally empty now. Each year, however, during the annual *Timkat* (Epiphany) celebrations, it is filled again.

Fasilidas had a grandson, regarded as possibly the greatest of the rulers of Gondar, Iyasu I, who gave the city yet another large castle decorated — in its day — with sumptuous ivory, gold and precious stones. It was described by a contemporary visitor as more beautiful than the house of Solomon and it is still a dramatic and beautiful building to behold.

There are many other castles and palaces to be seen in Gondar, but perhaps the finest sight that it has to offer is a church — Debra Berhan Selassie — which stands on raised ground to the north-west of the city. Built during the reign of Iyasu the Great, it is extremely well preserved. Its ceiling and interior walls are fantastically decorated with colourful religious paintings.

Lalibela

North-east of Gondar, and again accessible by a short flight from Addis Ababa, is Ethiopia's premier tourist attraction — the remote and ancient city of Lalibela with its eleven rock-hewn churches. King Lalibela, a twelfth-century monarch of the Zagwe dynasty, is credited with the creation of these churches. Their breathtaking execution — they were carved inside and out from solid rock — their treasures, and the priests who serve in them, are living expressions of the magnetic fascination of medieval Ethiopia.

125

During the season of the big rains from June through September, the town is effectively inaccessible as the airfield becomes waterlogged. A visit during Ethiopian Epiphany (*Timkat*, 18-19 January), or Christmas — or some major church festival in other months of the year — is particularly rewarding.

Axum

Axum, the site of Ethiopia's most ancient city, is accessible by means of a two-hour Ethiopian Airlines flight from Addis Ababa. There the seventeenth-century church of Saint Mary of Zion stands on the site of a much older church dating back to the fourth century AD. A small chapel annexed to Saint Mary's is said to house the original Ark of the Covenant.

Physically the most striking relics of Axum are its obelisks, or stelae, some still standing, some fallen. They are made of single blocks of granite carved in the representation of multi-storey buildings. The tallest, now fallen, stood over thirty-three metres high, weighed more than 500 tonnes, and represented a building of thirteen storeys. The biggest obelisk still standing is twenty-three metres in height, weighs some 300 tonnes, and has nine storeys. The carving is deep and precise, showing the beams for each floor and the windows, as well as a false door complete with knocker.

Other historical sites include the tombs of King Kaleb and King Gebre Maskal, the so-called Bath of the Queen of Sheba, and the ruins of a vast royal palace — near to the Gondar road. The market place, as well as souvenir shops, offer interesting curios and ancient coins for sale.

Harar

Finally, the medieval walled city of Harar in eastern Ethiopia is recommended to the visitor and may be reached, via the nearby town of Dire Dawa, in less than an hour's flight from Addis Ababa.

Harar was a fiercely religious city, dedicated to Islam, from the sixteenth century until 1887 when the authority of the central government was restored by Emperor Menelik. Even today, with its ninety-nine mosques, Harar is considered by many to be the fourth most holy city in the Islamic world. Sir Richard Burton's celebrated visit to Harar in 1855, when he found it harder to evade detection there than on his earlier visit to Mecca, nearly cost him his life. The poet Rimbaud also chose Harar as his place of exile from French intolerance.

The whole setting of medieval walls tightly embracing the ancient city, its rich market place — probably the most colourful in Ethiopia — its towering and majestic mountains, and its cool bracing air, make Harar an exciting place.